PRAISE FOR BE THE SWITCH

"Possibly one of the most frequent questions I receive as a pastor has to do with some aspect of discovering one's purpose for living. I'm thankful for a helpful resource to point people to in the future. Thanks, Jonathan!"

Ron Edmondson, pastor and author of *The Mythical Leader*

"Too many of us are simply existing but not truly living. Jonathan Pearson challenges each of us to wake up, pull back the curtains, take in the sunlight, and open up the windows to see and experience God's will and purpose for our lives. *Be the Switch* will both challenge and equip you to help your calling come alive, and immediately pursue the God breathed adventure of leading and living for more, right from where you already are."

Brad Lomenick, former president of CATALYST, founder of BLINC, author of H3 *Leadership & The Catalyst Leader*

"One of the most difficult things we face as Christ followers is discovering and living in our specific calling. Some of us over think it and some of us pay too little attention to it. But the great thing is, when we do discover our purpose, our calling, everything exponentially changes. Having clarity is powerful and freeing, and that's why I love what Jonathan has put together in *Be the Switch*. If you want to discover and live in your calling, read *Be the Switch* and make the impact you were meant to make."

Brandon Kelly, teaching pastor at The Crossing, co-founder of *RookiePreacher.com*, and author of *Preaching Sticky Sermons*

BE THE SWITCH

Living Your Calling While Living Your Life

Jonathan Pearson

Be the Switch: Living Your Calling While Living Your Life

ISBN: 978-1-948022-08-8

Rainer Publishing
www.RainerPublishing.com
Spring Hill, TN

Printed in the United States of America

To Melissa and Riley

You are my heartbeat. You make my job as a husband and dad so easy. Melissa, thank you for all you put up with. Thank you for teaching me about living a calling when you aren't called to be a "Pastor." Thank you for your patience, love, grace, and friendship.

Riley, you can't read this yet, but know how loved you are by your Heavenly Father and your earthly Father. You are a switch in this world who will lead and impact many. Never doubt that you are enough and that you have a purpose straight from your Creator. You are going to change the world!

To the Church

We are the church. Not those of us who are "professionals," but all of us who follow Jesus. Our impact is needed. Our calls are large. We have to live life pointing to grace and determined to be unified. We need each other, and the world needs us. In an increasingly dark world in need of Jesus's light, let's be the switch God needs us to be.

CONTENTS

FOREWORD

For too long Christians have fallen into the trap of thinking that calling only applies to those in full-time ministry.

What if that was not only a lie, but what if you're missing a calling you don't realize you have?

In these pages Jonathan Pearson seamlessly weaves between our world and biblical world, showing us how so many people who changed history almost missed their calling.

There is purpose and meaning in your day-to-day life. You have a calling. This book will help you realize once and for all that God's got far more planned for you than you think.

Carey Nieuwhof, founding pastor, Connexus Church

INTRODUCTION

To this you were called, because Christ suffered for you, leaving you an example, that you should follow in his steps. (1 Peter 2:21 NIV)

There are moments in life that are just . . . special. They become etched into our minds forever. Thinking about them brings a smile to our face. They are forever remembered as monumental and amazing.

For some, it's when they hit their first home run, got their first solo, wrote their first piece of music, read their favorite book, proposed to their girlfriend, or walked down the aisle. For others those moments are when they found out they were pregnant, got their dream job, or saw their first child enter the world. These are moments that no one can take away from us, not time or other memorable events.

I Have Several of Those Moments

One of those moments would certainly be when I asked my wife to marry me. I had developed quite the deliberate plan to propose in my own way, the way that I thought would be a little funny but extra special. I took my (then) girlfriend out the night after Valentine's for a very casual and uninspiring dinner. Afterwards, I brought her back to my apartment to watch some television. I had planted my roommate behind a door to come into the living room when I began to propose. He waited until the perfect moment so I could have the perfect photos of our engagement as it took place. I remember thinking, "How many people actually have pictures of the actual proposal?!" (Yes, this was before smart phones were the main camera we all use.) As we tried to find something to watch, my shaking hands put the remote down and felt under the couch where I had stashed the ring. I took the ring out, got down on one knee, and the look on her face burned into my mind forever.

Another of those moments was when we found out we were pregnant with our little miracle, Riley. We had been trying for years and were about to seek more help beyond begging God for a child.

We had already experienced many tearful months of hoping and then wondering what God was up to and why we couldn't have children. Then on Saturday morning I noticed she was taking a lot longer in the bathroom than normal. I walked into the bathroom and my wife looked me in the eye with happy tears in hers. That look burned into my mind forever.

Another one of these moments came years before I met my wife or thought of having children. It was when I clearly heard God's call on my life. I was thirteen-years old. It's been fifteen years, but I remember it like it was yesterday.

The church.

The song that was sung.

The look of the pulpit.

The green carpet under my feet.

The fall decorations hung in the church windows.

The smell of fall in the air.

I was a thirteen-year-old boy who already knew I wanted my life to count, really count. Not just to get out of high school and go away to college and work a job for forty years with a wife and couple of kids. Those things are great, but even then, I knew I was designed for more.

The sermon that Sunday night at my traditional

Baptist church had been about being light to those around you. I'm not sure what the pastor said, but I know what God spoke to me as we concluded the Sunday night service with the hymn, "Where He Leads Me." I stood to my feet, began singing, and immediately knew what God had said and that I either had to acknowledge it or I was going to hit the floor of this *Baptist* church. So right there, in my heart, I surrendered to the call of full-time vocational ministry.

It's changed my life ever since.

All of a sudden what used to matter didn't matter as much. What used to get me excited didn't cause quite the same excitement. What used to seem like a chore suddenly felt like a pleasure. The things that once consumed my thoughts and time no longer did.

That's what a calling does. It changes our perspective. It changes our goals. It changes how we spend our time, money, and energy. It changes what's fun for us and what isn't. It changes our priorities. It changes what time we get up in the morning and what we spend our day working on and thinking about.

A Call Changes All

A calling changes everything completely.

It can make washing windows seem like heavenly work.

It can make driving a school bus feel like preaching to thousands.

It can make sitting in a cubicle feel like the perfect place to be.

It can make taking orders and filling drinks feel like a means to a great end.

It can make answering calls a ministry.

It can make going to school a mission field.

It can make changing diapers and driving a mini-van as important as leading a Fortune 500 company.

A call changes all.

Several years ago, my family and I were on a day trip to Charlotte, North Carolina. On the way home, my five cups of coffee began to catch up with me. After having to go for what felt like hours, I finally found an exit with a gas station. Pulling off the exit, I noticed that this small town didn't have a "nice" gas station. All it had was the kind of gas station you don't want to go to after dark and kind of don't want to go to during the day either. Nevertheless, I had to go, so I had to stop. After hurrying inside and asking where the restroom was, the lady at the counter pointed me to the back corner. Seeing the sign in view, I walked hurriedly toward the door. When I opened the door, I was shocked! No, not the way you'd think, but I was shocked because the restroom was spotless. In all honesty, I don't' know if my bathroom at home is that clean. After using the restroom (yes, I washed my hands), I walked back toward the front of the store. As I was headed out the door, something told me to tell the lady at the cash register how good of a job she had done on the restrooms. As I began to compliment her, I still remember her words, "I know the Lord has me here, so I clean the bathrooms for Him."

Wow! That's a calling!

Go Ahead, Flip the Switch

Understanding our calling is a lot like flipping a light switch. Let me clarify with a little story. When my little boy was about two-years old, he came to me, as he often did, begging me to follow him into his room because it was dark. He didn't ever mind sleeping in the dark, but he didn't want to walk into a dark room. It would never happen.

So instead of flipping on the light and walking in, he came and grabbed me by the hand and pulled me into his bedroom so I could follow behind him as he turned on the light. It wasn't about me reaching the light switch; it was about his fear of even seeing the dark before the light came on.

Of course, I followed him in one day and he reached up to flip the light switch. As he did, the light turned on and it revealed the mess he had made in his floor earlier in the day. I'm glad he turned on the light; we could have both broken our necks!

After that day I started thinking about what that little light switch on the wall does. It seems insignificant enough. In fact, if you go to the hardware store, they're only a dollar or two. What they do, though, is a game changer. The light switch is what makes everything visible. It's what removes a little boy's fears and reveals the mess a daddy sees in his little boy's room. A light switch is the catalyst for change.

A calling from God to participate in his work is a call to be the switch, to be the catalyst in your neighborhood, school, family, classroom, boardroom, or office. It's a call to realize you have potential to be the switch and change the world around you.

Catch the Fire

Like a forest fire that rips through trees, brush, grass, and everything else in its path, my prayer is that this little book will make you destructive to the world. Not destructive in the "give me a sledge hammer" way, but destructive to the casual norms of society, the judgmental attitudes of the world, the darkness of the culture we live in. I pray you'll be destructive to the kingdom of hell as you learn to walk in the calling God's placed on your life.

I also pray that, like a fire, you'll be given life as you read this book.

One of the weird things about fire is that it can often bring life behind it. Have you ever seen people with lawns that look like they've been torched by a field of fire? They have. They burn their lawn so they can plant fresh grass that's unhindered by weeds and anything that could bring death. Our call is to bring life, to burn out the old things of death and to bring life to the people around us: the person beside us at work, the cashier at the grocery store, the friends we play football with or have band class with, the barista that knows our order when we walk in the door, the students in our classroom and the kids who call us Mommy or Daddy.

The only way we can be those people the way God wants us to, though, is by understanding our unique calling. This doesn't mean we surrender to the calling of full-time vocational ministry like I did at thirteen, but it means we start to do what we already do with a new motive and a renewed focus. Our calling is big, but it's also accessible enough to apply now.

Forest fires can be extremely destructive and are exceedingly dangerous to both humans and wildlife. Fire can also purify, such as when it kills germs during cooking. When you go to an undeveloped country, you'll see this principle at work. For those of us from the United States, the water in many countries isn't drinkable unless it's boiled first. The fire that causes the boil, while potentially deadly, is a source of life and renewal. We're called to be that to the people around us. To be salt and light, as Jesus would tell us, to the world and to help light the way for their sins to be cleaned in a miraculous way.

The Heart of This Book

As you make your way through this book, I want you to understand my heart. I'm a full-time minister, but my wife and the people I spend most of my time with aren't. I don't want them to do what I do, but I do want us all to understand that God has a call and a purpose on our lives that he desperately wants us to know and walk in. We are the body of Christ, and the Great Commission can't be left up to us "full-time" ministers and preachers. I love what I do, but I don't see the same people my wife sees at her job. If we're all inside an office or visiting people at the hospital or singing on a stage, much of the world will go unreached.

It's your call.

You can reach those people. It's urgent. It matters. That's why this book became a reality. It's reality because my heart is that we're all valuable agents in the Kingdom of God.

As You Read, Keep These Things in Mind

This Is Not a Step-by-Step Guide

We all hear God differently, we all find ourselves at different places in our walks with him, and we all discover our calls in unique ways.

God is a custom God. He customizes things to you. This book is simply one idea of how to walk in step with his call while you're walking your way through life, picking up the kids, working on the construction site, babysitting your grandbaby, or whatever else you do.

Reading a Book Isn't an Excuse for Not Listening to God

This book will give you principles to follow, to discern how God has uniquely gifted and called you to do his work. He could have chosen anyone, but he chose you to do this, as unqualified and unprepared and messed up as you may feel. He's called you. Don't, though, use the words in this book as an exemption from the words that come from the mouth of God. As you get started on his calling on your life, you're going to need to seek his face continuously. Long after you have put this book back on the shelf, you need to have your eyes in the Word and your heart focused on heaven. It's a continual process of hearing and obeying, listening and going, seeking and finding. I want to get you started, but he will keep you going. When things get tough and when your calling seems obvious but the results seem minimal, you'll need the voice of God. Keep seeking him.

Take Notes

I know you've heard it approximately 1,234,678 times, but it's true. What you write down (or type out), you're more likely to remember and practice. Get a highlighter, take some notes, jot in the margins, and do whatever else you may need to in order to take these key concepts away and into practice.

Sharing is Caring

Throughout the book, you'll see things that you believe are share worthy. Share away. Do we want you reproducing this book? No. That's not meaningful; that's a misdemeanor. Do we want you sharing on social media, discussing with your small group, and texting snippets to friends? Yes. Please!

So, are you ready?

Are you ready to do more than you thought you'd be able to do? Are you ready to be more? Are you ready to use your God-given gifts for the purpose they were given? Are you ready to let God use your problems for his purposes and your victories for his people? Are you ready to take your life from mundane to insane (okay, that was cheesy)?

Read on and do more!

CHAPTER ONE

THE CALL OF ALL

You did not choose me, but I chose you and appointed you so that you might go and bear fruit—fruit that will last—and so that whatever you ask in my name the Father will give you. (John 15:16 NIV)

You Have a Calling on Your Life

God desires to use you. You have purpose. Read that again. Let it sink in for a moment. You have a part in God's eternal purpose in the world.

Your life. Your daily routine. Your time from waking up to lying down. The 9-5. The errand running. The taxiing kids. The sitting at football practice. The teaching at the front of the class. The truck driving. The delivery making. The children chasing. The school going.

That time has a calling on it. As *believers, we're meant for more.*

You were meant for more than passing time.

More than getting by.

More than the next vacation.

More than making it through.

More than the weekend.

More than a paycheck.

More than average living.

My wife has changed jobs several times over the nine years we've been married. When we first got married, she worked for the Christian university we both attended and where we first met. She liked working there. It was safe. Her job was stressful at times, but she liked that she could talk about her faith anytime she wanted. Not only was talking about it acceptable, it was preferred. They wanted her to talk to her coworkers about what Jesus was doing in her life. They wanted her to talk to students about their faith as she helped them get enrolled and walked them through difficulties in their college life. The school even paid for her time to go to Christian conferences and the weekly chapel service that took place on campus.

About two years into our marriage we moved

to a new city and the drive to Melissa's old job at the university just became too far of a commute. She applied for jobs and eventually got one at the technical college in our small town. It was an extremely different atmosphere than her previous higher education job experience. No longer was it all faith, all the time; it was no faith, none of the time. Being a publicly supported college, she had to be really careful about discussing her faith, not because she was embarrassed, but because it was grounds for getting in major trouble.

I remember her coming home very upset one of the first weeks she worked at that technical college. It hit her that day that she was no longer in her Christian bubble and things were a little more difficult. She couldn't talk as openly about her faith. She came home that day and made a statement to me that still rings in my mind from time to time: "I just feel like I can't talk about God anymore. I feel like I can't do what I'm called to do."

After pausing and thinking for a second, I remembered something I had read years before about the kingdom needing people in the secular workplace. I began to explain to Melissa that she was sent into this new environment not to be silenced, but to find and operate in her calling. No longer was she around Christians all the time, but she was in a mission field five days a week. I reminded her to find her passion in her profession, to find her calling in her everyday.

So many Christians find themselves where my wife did that day. Not that they're in a new job or profession, but that they just don't know how to be used for Jesus where they are. You may find yourself in a place where you've settled into just surviving your job rather than succeeding in your calling. You may be trying to get through life when God has called us all to be effective in our lives. You may not even realize you have a call or that you can carry out your calling without becoming a preacher or a monk. Here's what I know: you'll never accomplish what you never see.

There's a little story in Scripture tucked into the story of Abraham becoming Isaac's father. That's kind of the blockbuster story, but a smaller, low-budget flick sits right alongside it: the story of Hagar and Ishmael after Abraham sent them away at Sarah's request.

Abraham had given Hagar some food and water and sent her and Ishmael on their way through Beersheba. They eventually ran out of water and were forced to find shade under a bush. As Hagar was just a little ways away from her young son, she cried out to God for something to drink. The

Bible says that at her most desperate moment, God "Opened Hagar's eyes and she saw a well full of water" (Genesis 21:19 NLT). It's amazing what we can find when our eyes are opened to the possibilities around us. It's surprising what wonderful things are provided for us when we see our current situation in a new light. So often, what happens to us is more about our perspective than our place.

You Have a Call, and It's Important

The term calling is often over spiritualized in church circles. A call comes directly from God, but it's not just reserved for the pastor on the platform, the musician on the stage, or the missionary in a foreign country. A calling, as defined by Miriam-Webster, is, "a strong inner impulse toward a particular course of action especially when accompanied by conviction of divine influence."

Did you catch that? It's something that comes from within and comes with conviction. It's something that we can't make up or force but comes from a much deeper source and place. It comes with a conviction that it not only *needs* to be but *must* be. Calling is divine. It's something that is placed in us by our Creator. Can our calling change? You bet you. Can the object of it change? Never. A calling's source is God, therefore, it's object is always him as well.

Think about the creation story as God created the things of the world? He created light, water, fish, and birds, then he moved on to what would be the pinnacle of his creation: human beings. As he knit the first man together, he said, "Let us make human beings *in our image*, to be like us" (Gen 1:26, emphasis mine. This is key because when we're made in someone's image, it means we have the same DNA. We have the same goals, longings, and Spirit as the living God. Since we are made in God's image, we're also made capable of reasoning, hoping, and producing. We're made to be agents of the One in whose image we're made. In other words, we have a calling because we have a Creator.

Paul talked a little about this to the church at Corinth in his first letter to them. Corinth was a corrupt place. Most scholars and people a lot smarter than me think it would have made our culture today seem like a church service. Needless to say, these believers had a lot of work on their hands. In 1 Corinthians 1:27 Paul writes to them and says, "But God chose the foolish things of the world to shame the wise; God chose the weak things of the world to shame the strong." Paul is saying, "Look, none of you were that smart, but that's okay because God uses everyone, regardless of how smart they are. He does it so he can get the glory, not the smart people."

God doesn't only use the people we'd consider most usable. He has a history of using average people to do amazing things.

Noah's Call Saved Creation

An average guy that God saw as faithful was called to do something crazy. He was called to build a boat to save humanity from a flood before anyone around him had ever seen the clouds open up and pour out rain. For the better part of what many think was one hundred years, Noah went to work on a boat with no water to justify his work. Noah wasn't a master boat builder or man of the water. He didn't own a pair of Sperry's or a shirt with a lure on it. He built the boat anyway. It took a while, but he completed the call even before he saw exactly why he was being called to do it.

Big callings from God often come with little

obvious reasoning. They can even come way before we feel like we're ready. Noah heeded God's call, and it saved his family and creation.

Abraham's Call Blessed Humanity

Abraham was an idol worshiper from a family of idol worshipers before God reached out and crowned him the daddy of us all. He was called to go, trust, believe, work, and be fruitful. He was called to go to a land that he had never seen to a destiny that he never knew.

He went.

He was promised to be the father of nations when he was way over what we'd consider child-bearing age.

He believed God and became the father of many nations.

Moses's Call Changed History

Moses's call was unique, unexpected, and he wasn't qualified for it. God chose Moses to lead the most amazing expedition in human history. Even though Moses was hesitant, had his ups and downs, and never fully accomplished the goal, he did complete the call. We'll look at him throughout the remainder of this book.

David's Call Transformed a Nation

A shepherd boy who was forgotten by his very own father became royalty who was known throughout history. He was faithful in the little things, so God knew he could trust him with more. David didn't just shepherd sheep, but he seemed to understand why he was to shepherd sheep. He wasn't a perfect man, but he is ultimately named as the main ancestor to our Savior. He walked. He stumbled. However, he was called.

Joseph's Call Fed a Nation

The outcast brother of twelve, Joseph had a dream. He was vocal about that dream, and it made his brothers jealous. He was thrown out, sold into slavery, threatened and brutally abused by people, but he was used by God. He eventually saved a nation from dying during a famine. The very thing the enemy had intended to kill him, led him to a place where he could be effectively used by God to accomplish a monumental calling.

John the Baptist's Call Paved the Way for the Savior of the World

"A voice calling out in the desert." (John 1:23). A man who was weird even for the times became a man known around Jerusalem and throughout history as the one who prepared people for their Rescuer to come. Some tried to follow him, but he always carefully diverted the attention from himself and onto his Savior.

Jesus' Call Rescues Sinners

A Jewish boy and son of a carpenter would construct the greatest love story in history. He was spotless, real, holy, and determined. He was human but God. He could have given up during the bruising and brutality of the cross. He could have aborted the plan. However, the plot of man was right in line with the plan of God, and Jesus lived out his calling. He died at the hands of some angry people but was able to turn the other cheek in the midst of the crowd's chatter. He was buried in a borrowed tomb and made the guards around his tomb look like careless children, as he made his way out on that first Easter morning. His call was complete.

Paul's Call Led to the Greatest Movement in History

Paul was an enemy of Jesus until Jesus made him a soldier of God. He was a top scholar of the school of hate. He was present as Christians were killed for being bold with their faith. He held coats for the greedy men who chucked stones at believers in Jesus. He was on his way to persecute more Christians when Jesus literally knocked him off his feet. The call was spoken, felt, and clear. It was obvious, large, and crucial. Paul answered and got to work. He journeyed across the Mediterranean through sweat, storms, and snakes. He sacrificed, gave, and loved at all personal costs. He wrote much of the New Testament, became the greatest church planter the planet has ever seen, and shaped the Christian faith as much as any other writer of Scripture. He withstood beatings, imprisonment, and shipwrecks. He survived it all and made an impact because he had a calling.

We Have a Call but We Run

One of the greatest things we can know and remember about God is that he doesn't call the qualified; he qualifies the called. To put it another way, he doesn't use the perfect; he knows how to use us all perfectly. Since he is our Creator, he knows us best. Like a chef can tell you the exact ingredients in their creation, God knows everything he's put in us and how he's wired us.

Do you remember how Moses's life began? It started out with him being a wanted man (or baby at the time). Remember, all the Hebrew women were supposed to have all of their baby boys put to death before they could grow up, reproduce, and further outnumber the Egyptians. Moses, however, was hidden for a few months by his mother. After she could no longer hide him, she made a desperate, Hail Mary attempt and put him in a basket just wishing on a prayer that someone would find him on his makeshift boat floating down the Nile. What happened? They found him alright. In fact, Pharaoh's daughter, the most powerful woman in the world, just happened to be lying out by the Nile one day and rescued little Moses from the basket. Moses grew up in the palace of Pharaoh and lived a cushy life . . . until he didn't.

One day, after he was grown up, Moses

witnessed some of his own Hebrew people being mistreated by an Egyptian, so he killed the Egyptian. To make sure the job was complete, he hid the Egyptian in the sand so no one would find out. They did, though. So Moses ran.

This is where many of us can begin relate to this story, isn't it? We may not have the cushy upbringing or have committed murder in the past, but chances are, we've run.

We've run from the thing that we fear. We've run from the thing that we really didn't fear, but that just made us uncomfortable. We've run from God and from our families. We've run from our insecurities by trying to cover them up with temporary solutions. We've run from our childhoods by trying to live through our own children.

It's what we do. We run, just like Moses.

What are you running from? Insecurities? Fear? A relationship? God?

Are you running from a calling? See, that's really what Moses was running from when he fled to Midian to avoid getting caught for the murder he had committed. He was running from the calling that had been placed on his life to lead the Israelites.

I believe many of us run from our calling. Maybe it's because we think that, like Moses, our past will disqualify us. Maybe it's because we've become comfortable with our status quo, day-to-day, safe life. Maybe it's because we think following God's call will mean we'll have to make a drastic change and cut our hair and learn chants and go vegan. We run, but we're called.

You Have a Call

What breaks your heart? What do you witness on a daily basis that makes you think, "Someone should do something about that," or "That's just not right!" What do you think about as you're working your job, going to your school, and living your life? What has your heart? What has God put there that doesn't seem to go away? What revives you? How has God knocked you off your feet like he did Paul? What has God spoken into your heart that burns to this very day?

Answering important questions can go a long way toward finding your calling. Searching your heart and knowing how you're wired will lead you close to your calling. That doesn't mean you'll have to quit your job, give all your money away, or eat vegan; it just means you'll have to refocus your current life and redirect your current goals.

We all have a call. Will you answer yours?

CHAPTER TWO

BE PRESENT ON THE FAR SIDE

For the eyes of the LORD range throughout the earth to strengthen those whose hearts are fully committed to him. (2 Chronicles 16:9 NIV)

You Can't Be Where You Refuse to Go

I read a story several years ago about the first women to ever make it to the North Pole. Basically, it all started when a lady named Caroline Hamilton was talking to a friend of hers who had been to the North Pole. While talking to her male friend, Caroline thought, "If he can do it, I can too."

The odds were stacked against her. The

expedition would be expensive and dangerous. To try to attract funding and some publicity, Caroline ran an ad in a local newspaper asking for people to help and for people to go on this journey with her. Her thinking, of course, was that if they split the costs and journey some, they'd have a higher probability to reach their goal.

Responses to the ad flooded in, so they met with the ladies who responded for a tryout of sorts. After selecting the expedition team, they decided to break up the journey into segments so no one lady had to do the whole thing. Through trials, deathly close encounters with animals, and bitter cold, they eventually became the first ladies to make it to the North Pole. They saw something that was far beyond what any of them could have ever dreamed and got to have their names stamped in history.

The tragic thing about that story for us? Many of us will never make it to our "North Pole" because we're unwilling to respond to the newspaper ad. We aren't willing to get to work where we are so we can accomplish the calling God has for us.

After all, being present and faithful where we are isn't what most people are sold these days, is it? Instead, we're sold in thirty-minute-or less segments, sitcom realities and romantic comedy timing. We're sold to climb our way to the top whatever it takes. We're told that if you don't have your own back, no one else will have it either. In fact, the current generation often fails to stay in a job longer than about two years. Why? Because we're sold that it shouldn't take long to rise to the top. When we don't make it in the timing we think we should, we blame it on our employer or someone who supposedly had it out for us, and we move on.

That's not the way it works with those things that are worth getting to, and that's not how it works with our eternally significant calling from God.

God Always Has a Purpose

The calling of Moses is one of the most significant passages in all of Scripture if we consider the significance it had on God's people. No, God doesn't always speak through a burning bush or ask us to take our shoes off (just leave those on for the sake of the people around you), but he does call us to be faithful where we are, to be the switch and shine light on those around us.

Just to recap the story of Moses in case you missed it earlier, we see early on in the book of

Exodus that a new king took over Egypt, where Moses's family was enslaved. The new king was basically tired of the Israelites growing in number and popularity, so he decreed that all male Israelite children be killed (Exodus 1:16). Now, don't skip over that part, because I think we can learn something from this extremely wicked king. For one, earlier in the chapter it says that he did not know Joseph and how Joseph had rescued the Egyptians from famine years previously. He didn't realize what had been done for him and his people and therefore didn't respect and honor the people who made it happen. We can all learn from this when it comes to our calling. We will never realize how vital we are to the church and to the kingdom of God if we forget what we were rescued from. If we forget that we were dead and are now alive, we'll fail to remember that our urgency should be high. Too many Christians today have forgotten what it was like to be dead and therefore sit on the sidelines of Christianity without making a difference or accepting a call to participate in God's plan.

We can also see from the king that pride and fear drive us to do incredible things. I know that times were different, but what this king issues is spurred by pride and fear. Pride that his people would be outnumbered and fear that the Israelites would change the country and his kingdom. Don't let pride and fear drive you away from the call God has on your life. Don't let how a friend does it or how someone used to do it keep you from doing it now. Don't let yourself believe that you're too "good" to do something when God has called you to serve and Jesus has modeled what that means.

Now, on with the story. The king issues the decree that all male children must die but soon realizes it's not having the effect that he'd though it would have. So he comes to the midwives who were delivering the babies and asks what's up. The midwives feared God and were therefore allowing these babies to live. Now, of course, they don't tell the king that, saying instead that the Hebrew women are quick baby deliverers. So the king gets a new plan. He decides that even if the male children are born, they are going to be thrown into the Nile and die.

Now, we know that this wasn't the case with Moses. Moses's mother hid him for three months after delivering him and then, when she couldn't hide him any longer, put him in a basket in the Nile and prayed for rescue. God rescued him. In fact, God blessed him doubly, as he was not only taken out of the river and adopted by Pharaoh's daughter, but Moses's mother was paid to take care of her own son by the time the story concludes. What an incredible picture of God's grace and protection!

After Moses grew up, he left Pharaoh's palace to spread his wings with other Hebrew people. One day, he was working and noticed an Egyptian beating a Hebrew. Enraged, Moses killed the Egyptian. Out of fear, Moses ran.

God once again displayed his grace to Moses and allowed him to meet his wife and have a child. Eventually, the angry and prideful king of Egypt died. The Israelites, with morale very low and what I'd imagine low faith as well, cried out to God to be rescued from their slavery. God heard their call and took notice (Exodus 2:25).

God noticed that his people needed rescue, and he was willing to act through Moses. Now, before we move on to the call of Moses, I want to concentrate on Exodus 2:25 some more. Let's read it again.

"God *saw* the Israelites, and He *took notice*" (Exodus 2:25 HCSB, emphasis mine).

When God sees a need on earth, he *usually* meets it with the help of people. When God's heart breaks, he searches for a person to fix what is breaking his heart. Isn't that amazing? Isn't it crazy? That the God of the universe, the One who made the stars, the sun, the moon, the oceans, the mountains, and the valleys, would use people to accomplish his purposes. The One who has the power to raise the dead and ascend to heaven uses you to do what it would seem he could easily do on his own.

Feel the weight of what is happening here at the end of Exodus 2. This is the birthplace of Moses's call, but it's also the beginning stages of ours. God bestows grace on us and others and accomplishes his purposes through his people. That means you have a calling for more, and it's toward people. That means our life is important to not just us but those around us.

Your calling is for more than what you're doing, at least the way you're doing it. What this means is that, with God, we can take our daily routine and give it reason. We can take our menial tasks and let them work miracles. We can use our career for the kingdom. We can focus our goals around his grace. We can be the switch and change things just because we adopt an attitude of significance toward what we're doing. We can be the switch and recalibrate why we do what we do.

The Far Side Doesn't Mean the Forever Side.

When we pick the story of Moses back up in Exodus 3, we find him tending sheep for his father-in-law, Jethro (Not the one from the classic television show, *The Beverly Hillbillies*, the other one). This is where many of us find ourselves today, isn't it? That's why many of you picked this book up in the first place. It may not be tending sheep, but you're doing something that, if you were completely honest, doesn't seem significant or sustainable. Sure, you're thankful for your job and your life (most days), but it's missing something. At the end of the day, it seems menial and mindless. It feels insignificant and irrelevant. Maybe it's something you've been doing for so long that you can't really imagine what else is out there, but you'd like to think there's something better. You've been faithful and always saw yourself doing what you're doing, but it's not because it's fulfilling you. You're there because you have to be. You're there because it's making a living for your family or it's the situation you found when you got married, or it's what your family did . . . so it's what you do. You're there, but you'd like to be somewhere else.

I was talking with a friend a while back who is

doing the family business of woodworking. He's been doing it since he was a little boy and he's now into his forties. As we were just catching up on our jobs and life in general, he made a statement to me that still rings in my head when I think about him or when I pray for him. He said, "This is what I do, but I'm not sure why I do it." Sound familiar? The truth is, what you do is important. Making ends meet is important. Providing for your family is important. Raising your children is a significant duty. It doesn't have to change completely, but the purpose behind it may need to change. The goal and passion of what we do can lead to us to regret our lives or to rejoice each day of our lives.

That's where Moses was with his sheep. In fact, in Exodus 3:1 we see that Moses is tending his father-in-law's sheep and he leads them to the "far side" of the wilderness. Isn't that where we often feel we are? We're on the far side of the wilderness. Sure, other people have a calling and are fulfilling their purpose, but they're not on the far side; they're on the side that can be used. They're preachers and pastors and super moms and principles of the school and bosses. We're none of those. We're on the far side of what God could use and is using.

To make matters worse, we're in the wilderness.

We're stuck, and no one really notices us. We're doing what wilderness people do: surviving. We're surviving on the weekend and vacation trips. We're surviving on our kids' football games and our next big purchase. We're surviving on getting home to watch Netflix or the game. We're on the far side of significance and just trying to survive in the wilderness. It's a lonely place to be.

The Value of the Far Side

The far side may be difficult and may seem meaningless, but there can be value in it. You see, Moses was tending sheep, but he was being faithful while tending those sheep. He was in a stinky business, but it was a business he stayed busy being faithful to.

That can be your story. That's what it means to be present. It may feel like we're in a meaningless place in life and at the far side of significance to God, but there can be value there when there's vision in our heart. When we're being faithful where we are and present in our situation, God can call us to more. He can make our place become more purposeful.

There's another story in Scripture of someone

who hung out with sheep all day and did so faithfully. A man named David would become the second king of Israel, but it started in the field. He'd eventually sit in a palace, but it started by being faithful in a pasture.

The prophet Samuel visited David's family after God told Samuel that the next king of Israel would come from David's family. After going through the family lineup, David's dad, Jesse, told Samuel, "Oh yeah, I do have one more son, but there's no way he's the one." Samuel insisted that someone go get David out of the field (where he was being faithful) and bring him in so Samuel could anoint him as the next king of Israel.

Samuel anointed David, and what did David do? He went back to the field with the sheep. He wasn't going to take the throne yet, so he did what he knew to do. He was a shepherd with a staff, but he was also a king with a calling. He shepherded with all his might, and it payed off a little later when he killed Goliath with a slingshot and a rock.

Moses and David have a lot in common. Both were faithful in their work. It wasn't too menial. It wasn't too little. It wasn't something they were just doing. They were faithful.

Being Present Leads to Finding Our Purpose

Exodus 3: 2 says, "Then the Angel of the Lord *appeared* to him in a flame of fire within a bush. As Moses *looked*, he saw that the bush was on fire but was not consumed" (HCSB, emphasis added). In other words, in Moses's faithfulness to tending sheep, God led him to his calling. Would Moses immediately give up sheep? No, but he would immediately get a calling to think about as he shepherded.

We see throughout Scripture a pattern of God not only using people who are faithful but of God clarifying their call as they are present and faithful where they are. That's what happened to Moses. Was God always with Moses? Yes. We saw that from the time he was born, but in this moment God is speaking to Moses a calling that would change everything he was going to do. The Angel of the Lord appeared to Moses in a real way.

You know what? Had Moses not been leading his sheep through the far side, he wouldn't have been at this bush at the right time. Would God have spoken to him somewhere else? Maybe, but not this same way. Not in this same manner and at this particular place. It was only in being present and engaged with a purpose in what he was doing that Moses gained a better understanding of his ultimate purpose.

So, Moses sees this bush and then notices that it's on fire but it's not burning up. It's funny because my three-year-old came home from church a few weeks ago and started telling me how he heard this story about Moses and wanted to know how this bush was on fire but not burning up. In these question-laden parenting moments, I usually do pretty good in giving honest but decent answers to a three-year-old's mind. This time, though, I had nothing. My response was, "Buddy, I have no idea." He dropped the conversation and moved on.

I don't want to just drop this conversation quite yet, however. You see, this is significant because, apparently, it wasn't that uncommon for bushes to burn in this setting. After all, it is the wilderness. It was uncommon, however, for the bush to burn and not to burn up. What was even more uncommon was God speaking from the midst of it. We'll talk more about that in the next chapter, but I don't want us to miss that God wants us to hear his call. He isn't into hiding himself or his word. He wants you to hear him. He'll use some pretty unique ways to get us to hear. For Moses, that was a burning bush, but for us it may be a sermon we hear, a

Scripture we read, or a situation life throws at us. Whatever it is, God isn't hiding, and he wants you to know how you can be faithful with a purpose where he has you right now. It's being present and purposeful at the same time.

God Isn't Hiding

It probably won't be through a burning bush, but God desires to speak. How do we hear Him? That's a loaded question that is different for everyone. I believe that God tailors his voice to you because he doesn't want to hide it. He wired you to learn and hear in different ways, and so he speaks in a unique way. I will say that, as we're faithful and present where we are, he'll begin to speak through circumstances about how he wants us to be faithful. He'll speak through his Word or through someone else.

One of the most influential people in my life is a man named Artie Davis. He was my pastor for years. I learned a lot under him. Perhaps the most valuable thing I learned was how to hear from God and that God does have an opinion for our situation. One of the things he taught me about hearing from God is that God often speaks in threes. He'll spark something in our heart, speak through Scripture, and confirm it through someone else. Or maybe he'll speak through someone, give us a heart nudge, and then confirm it through situations.

I don't know of anywhere in Scripture I can go to confirm this advice, but in my experience, it's solid. God speaks, and he wants us to know it. As we're present and listening, he's speaking. As we're willing to work at the far side and in the wilderness, he's willing to speak clear calling and wisdom into our lives.

Are You ready?

The far side is a tough place to be, but it's also the perfect place to be. It's where we can begin to be the switch. The far side is where we can get a passion for sparking something special in our circle and culture. It's the birthplace of something great if we're willing to go on over, press in, and seek God's voice.

CHAPTER THREE

GO ON OVER

Seek the Lord while he may be found; call on him while he is near. (Isaiah 55:6 NIV)

I hate traffic!

Can we just go on and get it out of the way and say that traffic is straight from Satan? Traffic is one of those things that I'm a part of, but I hate. I'm not a patient person. I never have been, and despite my greatest attempts I probably never will be. Traffic, combined with my lack of patience, makes for some trying times during my commute.

A year or so ago my family and I moved from a small town in rural South Carolina to one of the fastest growing places in the nation. I'm originally from the area we moved to, but things have changed so much. When you move, there are certain changes you always anticipate.

Things like daycare for your kids, school systems, incomes, where to go the gym, where to get your hair cut, where to get good coffee and Mexican food (at least for me), and a host of other things are usually on the list to figure out as you get ready to move. One of the things I overlooked before moving? Traffic.

Now, I guess I should pause and say that it's not terrible . . . most of the time. In fact, my friends from New York and parts of California often talk about how much they love the lack of traffic here. To me, though, the traffic is horrific.

One of those difficult traffic times got to me several months ago as I was turning left after getting gas in my truck. There was an open median in the middle of the four lane highway. Traffic coming from my left cleared, so I went ahead and got in the median to wait on the traffic coming from my right to pass by. I waited. Then I waited. Then I waited. When I got done, I waited some more. Finally, after what felt like ten minutes or so, I got enough room to turn into the closest lane.

I think many of us are in the median when it comes to our calling and being the switch in a world that desperately needs us to act like Jesus. We have Jesus living inside us, but we're stuck in the median, trying to decide what to do with this new-found hope and life. We're stuck between having accepted His grace, and sharing His grace.

Our Call Is Simple

One day Jesus was being quizzed by some folks who didn't like his style of teaching or his claiming to be the Son of God. To try to trap him between a rock and a hard place and force Him to choose to make parts of the Old Testament law more important than the others, a man came up to him and asked Jesus, "Hey, what's the greatest and most important of all the commands we follow?" Jesus, full of wisdom and grace responded with what's in Mark:

> "The most important one," answered Jesus, "is this: 'Hear, O Israel: The Lord our God, the Lord is one. Love the Lord your God with all your heart and with all your soul and with all your mind and with all your strength. The second is this: 'Love your neighbor as yourself.' There is no commandment greater than these." (Mark 12:29–31)

In the blink of an eye, Jesus summarized the entire law and issued a calling to every one of his followers. Our call isn't complicated. Our calling is to love God and to love others, and there's no opt-out clause. We have to do that. We have to make that turn and find tangible ways to live out this call Jesus places on our lives.

Our Calling Is Also More Specific

Our calling is simple: love God and love others. We all have that calling, but we also have a more specific calling on our individual lives as well. If the call to love God and others is the cheese pizza, our specific calling is the specialty pizza. In other words, a calling to love God and love others is the 30,000-foot view of the life God wants us to live. Like a pilot, however, we must eventually come down from the 30,000-foot view and connect with an exact coordinate. If a pilot misses the airport or is slightly off line, big and terrible things can happen. He must use his instruments, the air traffic control tower, the runway lights, and a host of other tools that I'm not going to pretend to understand in order to land in a specific spot and get where he needs to get.

Our calling is something we should eventually land on. We all have gifts, passions, ideas, backgrounds, thought patterns, and pasts that set us up to be used specifically by God for what he has for us. No one else can have the same specific calling you have on your life. God is so particular and cares so much about us individually that he tailors our call to us. It's how, right now, he desires for you to best love him and love others.

Moses Went on Over

Let's get back to the story of Moses. You'll remember from the previous chapter that he's out tending sheep when he sees this bush on fire but not burning up. If you think this is a little peculiar, you're not alone. Moses thought so too. In fact, in Exodus 3:3–4, it says,

> So Moses thought: I must go over and look at this remarkable sight. Why isn't the bush burning up? When the Lord saw that he had gone over to look, God called out to him from the bush, "Moses, Moses!" "Here I am," he answered.

As believers in Jesus who are seeking our call, we have to press in as well. God will often do something to get our attention to cause us seek his call on our lives. It may not be a burning bush, but maybe it's a passion that just isn't there anymore. Maybe God is trying to get you to press into him by giving you a passion that's never been there before, or you've had a child and it's sparked something inside of you. Maybe you just aren't as joyous as you once were, or maybe a family member was recently sick. Whatever the case, God often gets our attention with something big enough to make us say, "I need to go on over and check this out and see what it's about."

A Lesson from the New Testament

Many of the disciples received their calls to follow Jesus the same way. Matthew 4 tells us of the calling of James and John. They were, like Moses, going about their daily lives when Jesus called out to them. He made his presence known in the midst of their everyday lives. They responded. They went over. Matthew 4 goes on to say that James and John were in their boat with their dad, Zebedee. It says that after Jesus called out to them and got their attention, they "left the boat and their father and followed Him" (Matt 4:21).

Do you remember the story of the calling of Peter? It's one of my favorite stories in all of Scripture because there seems to be everything in it, including lessons about how God calls us to follow him and to be used by him.

The calling of Peter appears in both Matthew's and Luke's Gospels. Luke 5 is a more descriptive view of what happened when Peter decided to jump ship on his life and follow Jesus. The story begins with Jesus doing some teaching along the shore of a lake, where a large crowd was gathering. People kept coming as he kept teaching. Finally, the over-capacity crowd begins to make more room by pushing towards the front. Jesus keeps backing up toward the lake and eventually gets so close to actually being in the lake that he decides to go with plan B. Plan B was to borrow a boat and head out into the lake himself, so he wouldn't take up any of the room the crowd so desperately wanted. He hijacks a boat (kind of), which just happens to be owned by a guy named Peter.

After Jesus finished teaching, he tells Peter to go into deeper water and, after some reluctance, some of which was because these professional fishermen had fished all night and caught nothing, Peter decides to oblige Jesus. The Bible gives a beautiful picture of what happened next in Luke 5:6–11

> When they had done this, they caught so many fish, their net started to break. They called to their friends working in the other boat to come and help them. They came and both boats were so full of fish they began to sink. When Simon Peter saw it, he got down at the feet of Jesus. He said, "Go away from me, Lord, because I am a sinful man." He and all those with him were surprised and wondered about the many fish. James and John, the sons of Zebedee, were surprised also. They were working together with Simon. Then Jesus said to Simon, "Do not be afraid. From now on you will fish for men." When they came to land with their boats, they left everything and followed Jesus.

Do you see the significance of that? Peter had heard Jesus preach and seen him work, but it was when Jesus did something that caught Peter's attention that he decided to follow and begin his calling. Peter wasn't poor or friendless or a guy with nothing to do. Peter was a fisherman called by Jesus and willing to press into that calling. He left everything he had to follow Jesus and the call Jesus had for his life. In fact, Peter would continue to fish. His fishing was now for people.

What about You?

Are you willing to go over to the bush and seek your calling and begin doing what God's called you to do? Are you like Peter? Are you willing to go a little deeper and see Jesus do something great so you can begin walking in your calling? The truth is, it's easier if we don't. It's easier for us to continue living a menial, average Christian life, to go to church occasionally, say a prayer every now and then, and stick in our routine. It's easier not to press into all that God has for us. It's easier, but it's not best.

Like Moses, Peter, and the other disciples, God has a calling he wants you to hear. He has an assignment that needs your attention. He has a difference he wants you to make.

Are you listening? Are you seeking him on the far side and pressing into him as he is seeking to get your attention? Are you willing to leave where you are and what you know in order to gain something so much more fulfilling and purposeful? Are you willing to press into the voice of God and understand how you can do more of the same but in a way that means more?

Will someone else do it if you don't? Probably. Will you miss so much of the freedom and purpose and joy God has for you if you don't? Absolutely.

God is working; we have to go on over and join him.

CHAPTER FOUR
UNDER THE LIGHTS

But you are a chosen people, a royal priesthood, a holy nation, God's special possession, that you may declare the praises of him who called you out of darkness into his wonderful light. (1 Peter 2:9 NIV)

I love spicy foods.

Let me be clear. I'm not one who likes spicy stuff just for the heat. I'm not the one to enter a wing challenge and have my tongue burned off trying to eat the super-duper torch sauce. I do, though, like spicy stuff with flavor. Mexican food is my kryptonite, and hot sauce belongs on just about anything. From tacos to eggs to pinto beans, hot sauce is my favorite food group for sure.

I like putting hot sauce on food after it's cooked, but I also like cooking with it. One of the traditions my wife and I have adopted since we moved last year is that whoever gets home first usually starts dinner while we're waiting on the other one. Of course, she's the better cook, but I like to pretend that I know what I'm doing, so when I get to start dinner, I always through extra ingredients into whatever it is we're having. I add whatever spices kind of smell like they belong. I add garlic to just about everything, and I love adding hot sauce. My wife doesn't mind stuff being a little spicy, so I usually give a splash or two to whatever we're having, especially soups.

Not long ago, I got home first and started the soup. We had prepared it mostly in the slow cooker the morning of, so my job was just to stir it and see if it needed anything extra. My extremely scientific taste test done with my trained palate demonstrated that it needed hot sauce. I thought for a second about what kind of hot sauce and decided that sriracha was definitely the way to go. After a few squirts from the bottle, I put the lid back on the slow cooker, flipped it on warm, and waited for her to get home.

When she got home, I put some in a bowl and served her. I put some in a bowl and went to eat myself. As soon as I sat down, I heard a spitting and gagging sound coming from my wife. She started looking around for something to drink. Of course, I had forgotten that part and made a beeline for the fridge to get her something cold. After the pain subsided, she gently informed me that I may have used a little too much sriracha in the soup (or a lot too much).

Spice It Up

As Christians, I think we're called to be somewhat like hot sauce in soup. No matter what bite you eat or where you go, we're called to blend in but also stand out. Melissa had no idea I had put that much hot sauce in the soup (I didn't either, really) until she tasted it and was around it. Isn't that our call? To be in the world but not of it? To be salt and light?

Do some research on hot sauce and it won't take you long to see that hot sauce is made of only a few ingredients, usually vinegar, water, and peppers. The odd thing about peppers is that, usually, the smaller they are, the hotter they are. For instance, a jalapeño is hotter than a bell pepper. The bell pepper may look hotter and meaner on the outside, but the jalapeño is what will give you the punch.

That kind of sums up what God does with us, doesn't it? We blend in but stand out. The small among us are called big in the kingdom of God. Those of us who think we have little or nothing to offer actually give a lot when we're submitted to God. Often times God uses the lowly and the perceived weak to change the world. He uses the ones most people would throw out, to show out, for his sake.

To Be Light, We Have to Be Under the Light

I have a ton of electronic devices. Maybe a few too many. I'm typing this on an iPad with my phone and Mac sitting here as well. Because it's just where he left it, my son's iPad is sitting beside me also. I'm listening to music on Bluetooth headphones. I have a TV remote that requires programming and charging. The thing about all of those electronic devices is that they aren't any good without being charged. Oh, I have chargers everywhere. I have chargers by my bed, in my office, by the sofa, and in the car. Nevertheless, my electronics still get drained and the battery meter still gets to 0 percent.

Like those electronic devices to which I may or

may not be addicted, we as believers aren't good at radiating Jesus without living under the light of Jesus first. In other words, we have a limited ability without the glory of Jesus radiating through us. To quote the old country church sign, "We need to lay out in the Son."

A Little-Known Example

Do you remember King Josiah from the book of 2 Chronicles? He's listed in Matthew 1 as being in the lineage of Jesus, but we don't hear a ton of sermons based on his life. He is, however, a significant character in the Bible. Josiah was king after his granddad and dad, who it just so happens, were some of the most wicked kings in the history of Judah. They completely abandoned everything King Hezekiah and previous generations had fought so hard for. It even got to the point where they not only worshiped other gods than the true God, but they started borrowing gods from other religions. They were seeking something so bad, they couldn't' even find it in their own country.

After all of this wickedness, King Josiah takes over the throne after his father is assassinated just two years into his kingship. The problem was that

Josiah was only eight-years-old. Yeah, you read that right. He was king at eight. At eight, I'm pretty sure I was catching fireflies in my backyard and laughing at poop jokes. Here's Josiah taking over as king. Now, he wasn't necessarily calling the shots at this point, but he was king nonetheless.

Second Chronicles 34:3 reads, "During the eighth year of his reign, while he was still young, Josiah began to *seek* the God of his ancestor David." Four years after this, Josiah would begin to clean things up in Judah. He'd go on to destroy the gods they had resurrected and cleanse the temple. While renovating the temple, workers would find the Book of the Law, and revival really broke out. Unfortunately, Josiah's life didn't end well, but his impact was felt.

Before Josiah led revival, though, he lived under the Light, seeking God. You see, as we seek God, he begins to give us a burden for what's broken around us. As we live under the light of Christ, our minds are shaped by him. We begin to see others as he sees them. We begin to have our hearts broken by what breaks his. We begin to discover who we are in him. We begin to gain passion for what he's put in us. In order to be light, we have to live under the light.

Moses Pressed in Too

In the Exodus 3 passage we've been looking at, verse 4 says, "When the Lord saw that he [Moses] had gone over to look, God called out to him from the bush, 'Moses, Moses!'" Do you see the progression of this? Moses is tending sheep as he was accustomed to doing, God appears in a burning bush, Moses goes over, and God begins to speak as Moses presses in. That's the way it often works for us too. The thing that often makes it harder for us is the distractions between the time God gets our attention and we begin to move closer to him and live under the light. Culture can get so confusing and so loud that our call can be harder and harder to hear. Moses experienced this in a field; we experience it on busy city streets. We must, however, press in as he calls out to us from our daily life.

It's a Fight

Ultimately, we have to fight to be light. We have to fight to press in with all the busyness surrounding us. With all of the lies that are whispered to us as we begin to press into God and seek his calling, it can be easy to lose passion quickly. God births something in us and life seems to suck it out of us. We feel like we're moving forward on what God is wanting us to do and someone says something to us that throws us off track.

It really is a fight to remain pressed into God and hear him as he calls. Going back to the story of Josiah, can you imagine what the people around him whispered to him? I'm sure they told him it wasn't worth it. I'm sure they told him that he came from a line of wickedness and that there was no use in seeking God and going after his calling. I'm sure he was hit with whispers of being too young or too inexperienced to follow a call. He fought anyway.

What Do I Do?

Exodus 3 goes on to give us insight into the conversation between Moses and God. In verse 5 God says, "Do not come closer. Remove the sandals from your feet, for the place where you are standing is holy ground." God continues, "I am the God of your father, the God of Abraham the God of Isaac, and the God of Jacob." This obviously overwhelmed Moses because the end of verse 6 says that Moses "Hid his face because he was afraid to look at God." Can you imagine? Here, Moses has gone from man on the run to man speaking with the Creator of man. Moses should have been dead by man's command but is called based on God's plan.

Exodus 3 continues, "Then the Lord said, 'I have observed the misery of My people in Egypt and have heard them crying out because of their oppressors, and I know about their sufferings" (Exod 3:7 HCSB)." I think that is an important verse because we see God speaking the burden directly into Moses. At this point Moses didn't know exactly what he was being called to do, but he knew the burden because God had spoken it into him.

Do you know your burden? What is the thing that you see and believe someone should do something about? What is the thing that breaks your heart when you encounter it? The thing you think must be, you must do? That's the burden. Maybe it's the way you parent. Maybe it's your own children or spouse. Maybe it's your local elementary school or someone at work. Maybe the burden God is speaking into you is your classmate, your retirement home, or your team. That's the burden.

Where Do I Start?

My wife and I have moved about six times now over our ten years of marriage. Every time we move, it kind of goes the same way. In the weeks leading up to moving, she does the packing. The job is so overwhelming to me, she knows now to just let me help on my own timetable. So she packs, and I kind of walk around like a lost puppy. I hate for things to be out of place, and so I kind of hold on to one room each time as we (she) pack.

Once we have everything in boxes and moving day approaches, we always have somewhat of the same conversation. It's one of those conversations that you'd think I'd mature out of, but she always has to have it. It's the me panicking about the work and her talking me down from just leaving it all and buying new stuff. My problem with moving and packing a box or a truck is that I don't know where to start. The job seems so big that I'm often frozen in my tracks and overwhelmed at what lies ahead. The conversation usually ends with her reminding me that I just have to start somewhere if we're ever going to get anywhere.

That's the way it is in following our call as well. When you have a burden, you don't always have an outlet or a process. When you have a purpose, you don't always have a plan. Do you remember Abraham's call in Genesis 12 to go to a land God would show him? God told him to go without telling him the destination. With our calling, we're often given the burden but not told where to go right away. So we have to just start if we're ever going to accomplish it.

Moses's conversation with God kind of hits a climax in Exodus 3:10 when God tells him, "Go. I am sending you to Pharaoh so that you may lead My people, the Israelites, out of Egypt." Moses is told just to go without the plan. Moses has a burden and a command to go, and that's where we are as well.

How to Get Started

Moses will get more instructions as he walks with God over the next few verses, but for us, where do we start when it comes to our call? How do we become the switch and initiate change around us? We have to start somewhere, but where?

Start with what's in front of you. I know that seems like I'm questioning your intelligence, but it's true. You have to start with the opportunities you're given. Opportunities come and go every day that we miss because we aren't living under the light and because we aren't thinking about being the switch in our world. Opportunities to help someone lift something out of their car, return the cart to the store, or pick up something they've dropped. Opportunities to honor our coworkers when everyone else is dishonoring, chances to go above and beyond when we don't have to, and opportunities to give financially often pass by without getting a second thought. We're asked to serve at church and instead of trying it as we discover our calling, we turn it down because it isn't exactly what we want to do.

To begin living out our calling, we have to start. We have to begin with what's close to our heart as well. Often times God will not only give us a burden, but he'll also give us an avenue near our heart. In other words, we may have a burden for the homeless, but God will give us a certain homeless shelter that seems to mean something special to us. Or we'll have a heart for our coworkers and God will give us a way to garner more influence with them.

I heard the story of how the stethoscope was invented. It appears that the stethoscope was invented somewhat on accident. There was a doctor who got tired of trying to listen to the hearts of his patience by putting his ear up to their chest and so he started trying other methods. Eventually he placed some rolled up paper tubing between their heart and his ear, and the stethoscope as we know it was born. That's how it works. We have a burden and then we see the avenue to make a way to it. First, though, we have to get started.

Not Alone

We are not alone. As God was with Moses, he is with us. We'll spend our entire lives under the light of Jesus, but we have to walk as the light as well. Are you ready? Have you started pressing into God and developing your burden? Have you started getting busy with what's in front of you? I hope so, because the rewards are great!

CHAPTER FIVE

IT COMES FULL CIRCLE

But he gives us more grace. That is why Scripture says: "God opposes the proud but shows favor to the humble." (Jas 4:6 NIV)

Meet in the Middle

Until a year or so ago, my wife and I lived about two hours from our child's closest grandparent. As you can imagine, that made free child care scarce at best. There was no such thing as grandma or grandpa coming over for the evening to watch our little man while we had some together time at a local restaurant. Instead, we either had to take him with us or plan for him to be gone a couple of days to make the drive to one of his grandparents' homes worth it.

Fortunately, neither set of grandparents made us drive the entire two hours by ourselves. Instead, we worked out places to meet them that were about half way between our two homes. A two-hour trip both ways sure made it much easier than a two-hour trip one way to get a little free time. It's always easier when things work both ways and meet in the middle.

Moses Moans . . . And So Do We

Moses received his instruction from God. He had his call in the palm of his hand. He was to go to Pharaoh and free the Israelites from the bondage of slavery that had long held them back and that they had long desired to escape.

If we stopped right there, it would make it seem as if God was all about himself. Rightly so, but nevertheless God would seem like a chess player with pawns on a board. Thankfully for Moses's sake and for ours, that's not who God is. God is much more gracious, loving, and thoughtful than that.

God called Moses to go. Like many of us who are wrestling with our calling and being the switch in our lives, Moses had some doubts about going to Pharaoh. Isn't that where many of us are today? We know that we're called to do something more than just the 9–5, but we have doubts about that calling and our ability. We want to be people who go and are the light that God's called us to be, but the doubts hold us back. If it's not doubts, it's fear. If it's not fear, it's insecurity. That's where Moses obviously had an issue, because he said in Exodus 3:11 (NIV), "Who am I that I should go to Pharaoh and bring the Israelites out of Egypt?" Imagine, here's Moses who was just kind of doing his thing and all of a sudden is confronted with a burning bush that isn't burned up. He begins to press into God, and all of a sudden God is telling him to come face-to-face with the most powerful man on earth at the time. Even more so, God tells Moses to command this man to let the people go who have been basically providing much of the work force for the nation.

Moses obviously feels incapable of being the spokesperson for his people and for God. He has his doubts. Doubt is the enemy of purpose and progress. Many of us have allowed doubt to cripple and prevent us from doing anything significant for God. Sure, we've heard the whisper of God in our lives to go and do something different or change how we're doing what we're doing, but we feel insignificant and doubt begins to cripple us.

Who are you doubting when it comes to your calling? It may feel, as it did to Moses, like you're doubting yourself. It may seem that you're doubting your ability and talents, but really it comes down to doubting God. Sure, we'll never put it like that, but we're really doubting that God has given us gifts. We're really doubting that God will hold up his end of the bargain. We're really doubting that God will move the rest of the pieces it seems he'll have to move, if we're going to accept his calling on our lives. We're really doubting that we'll switch on the light he's called us to be.

It's All in Who You Know

Whether we doubt or not, I believe God is telling us the same thing he told Moses in Exodus 3:12: "I will be with you." Do you feel the weight of that? As we move to a place of greater understanding and as we go in the power he has given us, we aren't by ourselves. The One who calls us is faithful to walk with us. The One who tells us to go is never willing to leave us gone by ourselves. Knowing God is with us means that even when we doubt ourselves or him we can move forward because of who's with us.

I have a three-year-old son (please pray for us!). He loves independence until it's something he is scared of or just doesn't understand. For instance, one Saturday afternoon I took him to breakfast. It's kind of become our thing, to get breakfast on Saturday mornings while my wife has a little alone time. This particular breakfast Saturday, we went to a local fast food chain to eat a biscuit and talk about life (as much as you can with a three-year-old who really just wants to watch Handy Manny). When he saw the place I get my haircut out of the window in the shopping center behind the restaurant, he decided he wanted a haircut that morning. As much as I tried, I couldn't talk him into waiting until the next week; he really wanted a haircut. As we left the restaurant and drove to the haircut place behind it, he was excited about having his haircut and eating a lollipop after it. As we got out of the truck, he was still excited. As we walked into the place and he heard the trimmers and saw the hair falling, he suddenly got less excited. I didn't have to drag him into the chair, but I did everything but that. Finally, I told him that I'd get a haircut in the chair next to him at the same time. After a few seconds of thought, he agreed to sit in the chair if I sat beside him. A haircut seemed overwhelming until he realized that I was with him.

I believe there are countless Christians who are, like Moses, in place to do something great but have failed to realize that they don't have to do it in their own power or by themselves. That, in fact, they don't even have to do it at all. They aren't responsible for the outcome; they're just responsible for the obedience. God's job is the success; ours is the surrender. That's what God told Moses, and that's what he's telling us today. Our calling isn't all up to us; it's just for us. Our calling isn't just us reaching out for God; it's God reaching back to us.

Another Great Calling Realized

One of my favorite stories in all of the Old Testament is the calling of Abraham. Yeah, many people love the story of him and Sarah having Isaac, but I love the calling he endured before any of that could happen. Abraham's story begins when he was still Abram in Genesis 12.

> The Lord had said to Abram, "Go from your country, your people and your father's household to the land I will show you. "I will make you into a great nation, and I will bless

> you; I will make your name great, and you will be a blessing. I will bless those who bless you, and whoever curses you I will curse; and all peoples on earth will be blessed through you." So Abram went, as the Lord had told him; and Lot went with him. Abram was seventy-five years old when he set out from Harran. (Gen 12:1–4 NIV)

The thing I love about those verses is that this wasn't the first time God tried to call Abram. In fact, God had spoken to Abram before his father died; God told him to go then, but Abram failed to do so. I love that because it means that Abram (Abraham) wasn't perfect. He missed the call too, but God was gracious and called again. It also means that God can use those difficult times in our lives to reveal new things to us. Abram was dealing with his father's death when God spoke this word into his life. This is the word that would ignite Abraham's legacy as the father to all nations. What difficult thing in your life is God using? What is he speaking to you in the midst of tragedy, discontentment, or uncomfortable surroundings. Is his call going out to you again in the midst of the job you hate, the people you're tired of, or the struggle you're in?

Another thing I love about the beginning of Abram's call is the promise of God in the four short verses listed above. In fact, depending on the translation we read, we could read the word "I" as many as seven times in the first seven verses of Genesis 12. What God is saying to Abram and what he's saying to us as we step into our calling is, "It's for you, but it's on me." In other words, God is telling us that if we'll surrender, he'll deal with the results. If we'll be willing, he'll make us able. You don't have to worry about the doubts, insecurities, failures, or lies of the enemy when the Creator of the world is calling you out and going before you.

It's Just the Way It Works

Jesus delivered the most famous sermon ever in the Sermon on the Mount. Basically, it was a spontaneous church service that Jesus decided to lead one day as the crowds followed him. He found himself on a mountain side with these crowds of people around him, so he sat down for a teaching moment.

The Sermon on the Mount is the most famous sermon ever, and it wasn't live streamed, live tweeted, or quoted on Instagram. It's famous because its words are timeless. In the middle of this sermon, Jesus is teaching on worry and utters one of his best quotes ever, "But seek first his kingdom and his righteousness, and all these things will be given to you as well" (Matt 6:33 NIV). Since his sermon, this quote of Jesus has appeared on many Instagram photos and even cross-stitch pillows (remember those?) around the world. In this part of his sermon Jesus is trying to get us to understand that our seeking God and following in his footsteps is all the setup for success we need. In other words, when we begin to seek him and walk in the calling and gifts he's given us, he takes care of us and our shortcomings. When we take the step of faith to live differently, work differently, parent differently, teach differently, and lead differently, he takes care of the rest. That quote is true for us who are trying to be the switch and shine light on things around us.

Don't' be afraid to go. Like Moses will later understand, God never leaves those he calls. He never forsakes those that love Him. He never abandons those He asks great things of. Thankfully, he's called us all, loves us all, and asked us all to do great things through his power and plan. We aren't alone, and we aren't in our own strength. We aren't on an island, and we aren't unprepared. Like Moses and like Abraham and the rest of the people God has used greatly throughout history, we go and he gives as we need.

CHAPTER SIX
DON'T GET TOO COMFORTABLE

Since we live by the Spirit, let us keep in step with the Spirit. (Gal 5:25 NIV)

Things change.

Not long ago, I remember going to the gas station and getting a Diet Coke and believing and even hearing other people tell me that I made a healthy choice. The first thing people would commit to when trying to lose weight was drinking more water and drinking diet soft drinks instead of the calorie filled real-sugar ones. On top of that, they'd look for all the fat-free snacks they could find. We all believed that some things would make us slimmer while others would make us bigger. I distinctly remember buying bags and bags of gummy bears because the bag said "fat free" on the front.

Fast forward just a few years (I'm not that old), and everything's changed. They say that artificial sweetener found in diet soft drinks actually makes us bigger and makes us crave sweeter foods and more foods. Fat is no longer all bad, and some of it is even recommended for weight loss. Avocado prices are soaring because people have discovered the health found in the fatty vegetable (or is it a fruit?). We no longer count fat grams but rather calories and carbohydrates (I think). Protein—even bacon—and eggs are good again.

Things change.

A Godly Bother

What bothers you? I don't mean what kind of gets on your nerves in the same way your brother or sister did when you were younger. I don't mean who's that coworker who always seems to find the last nerve you had left and grinds on it all Monday long. I mean, what bothers you?

You see, as I look through Scripture I see the people God used the most were the people who had a burden for what they saw was broken around them. That's what made them be the switch. They saw something that needed to be illuminated in their world. They felt the call from God. They ran with endurance and passion toward the burden that bothered them.

Moses's Burden Led to His Calling

Let's continue looking at the call of Moses. As we've said previously, Moses was an ordinary guy in whom God birthed a calling. God gave Moses his burden early on. God gives us burdens as well. Look at Exodus 3:7–8 (NIV):

> The Lord said, "I have indeed seen the misery of my people in Egypt. I have heard them crying out because of their slave drivers, and I am concerned about their suffering. So I have come down to rescue them form the hand of the Egyptians and to bring them up out of the land into a good and spacious land, a land flowing with milk and honey.

Did you catch that? God was burdened, and so he calls a man. That's being the switch. God births the idea of his burden into Moses. God continues,

> So now go. I am sending you to Pharaoh to bring my people the Israelites out of Egypt. (Exod 3:10 NIV)

The burden was felt and then Moses was called. God still works the same way. He is burdened and he births it in us. Let that sink in for a moment. God uses us to fix and work in his burdens. He uses us to bring about change in the very world that he created.

What Shapes a Burden?

My son is now almost four. That's hard to believe! It's been somewhat of an up and down five years total with him (including the whole pregnancy thing). You see, early on my wife and I knew that we were classified to have an at-risk pregnancy. She had some medical issues that we knew would make it hard for Riley to be carried to full term. For the first seven months or so of the pregnancy, we'd see specialized doctors who would check on Riley's status to make sure he was growing and gaining weight. They checked the baby and my wife regularly to be sure that he would be in the womb as long as possible. About two months before his due date, we thought our prayers had been answered when the specialists released us from the weekly tests because they believed that the way things were looking guaranteed a close to full term baby.

The week after the doctor so kindly released us, I came home from work to find my wife in the fetal position on the floor in pain. She assumed it was some pain with the pregnancy, but I knew that there was something more. We called the doctor and rushed to the hospital. About 10:00 that night the doctor came into our hospital room and said that she had had a few contractions but they had done a test and were 99 percent certain that she wouldn't have Riley within the next few weeks. They decided to keep us overnight so we wouldn't have to worry about making the long drive back home that night. About 2:00 the next morning, Melissa's water broke and we had to have an emergency C-section.

The next few weeks would be up and down as Riley was in the NICU, hooked up to every machine imaginable. In the end, we were extremely blessed. During those weeks in the hospital he never took a real step backward and is one solidly built and healthy (almost) four-year-old today.

What happened during those experiences with

him, though? We developed a burden for premature babies and at-risk moms. A year after Riley's birth, my wife helped raise money for organizations that cater to premature babies. Suddenly, it meant something more. It just means more when we've lived it, breathed it, and have the scars to prove it. It means more when it's close to home.

Moses had the same kind of close relationship with his burden and calling. In fact, if we rewind his story a little, we see that he actually kills an Egyptian because of what they're doing to one of his own people. I'm not condoning killing people you think are mean to you or your family, but we certainly see that his burden was close to home. So when God called Moses and gave him his burden, his surroundings, connections, and past help propel that burden into a calling. He was willing to be the switch because he knew what the light would do and where it would cause change.

That's the thing too, isn't it? We're so much more likely to do something when we see that it is going to make a difference and we're tied to it at our core. One of the greatest examples of this is the story of when Daniel was picked to be one of King Nebuchadnezzar's prized men. The plan was to choose a few men to become some of the king's finest. For three years, these Israelite men would be taught the Babylonian way and eventually appear before Nebuchadnezzar. They were to learn the customs, traditions, and language of the Babylonians. They were to eat the same foods as the royal court. Only, Daniel had a burden not to eat foods that went against his Jewish tradition. So Daniel used that burden and his background to help him stand up to the men who would train him. He asked to eat the foods he was convinced and convicted to eat. Sure enough, as we know the story, the experiment worked. The men who ate the diet Daniel brought forth were the healthiest of all. All because Daniel used his burden and his convictions the way God called him to at that moment.

When Burdens Become Callings

I still remember where I was when I knew that I was called into vocational ministry. I had always wrestled with the idea and believed I was called, but I distinctly remember when it became real.

It was my senior year of high school, and I received a phone call no teenager ever wants to take. It was late one night when a friend called me and told me that my best friend had been killed in a car accident that evening. This friend and I had gone to preschool together, gone on double dates together, and even gotten into some trouble together. We were best friends in every aspect of the word. Like any best friend, his mom had kind of become my second mom as well. I had dinner at their home frequently and still remember the taste of her homemade spaghetti sauce that would have made even the finest Italian cooks pat her on the back. The night that I got the call, I got in my car and hurried to their home. As I knocked on the front door and was let in by a family member, I still remember the look in his Mom's eye when she saw me. It was a look of hopelessness, of terror, of grief. It was also one that made the Spirit clear to me that I was called to comfort and help people. I was called to be a full-time pastor.

You see, the relationships we have and the burdens we develop and the people we love aren't put into our lives by mistake. You may think that that family member you can never get along with or that situation you're dealing with is just happening by chance and you wish it'd go away. It's not just by chance. It's developing something in you. A burden is being birthed that will turn into a calling. Much like my wife and I now see premature babies from another perspective, and much like my painful experience with death solidified my calling, your burden is pointing to your calling. It's beckoning you to do something about it.

Burdens Change, So Callings Change

We can't stop at the burden though. If we continue to look into the life of Moses, we'll see that he had multiple callings on his life. Sure, he was called to go to Pharaoh in the famous "Let my people go," passage, but his calling also evolved as he obeyed. His burden evolved as well.

Change Like Clay

Many people don't know the story of how Play-Doh came to be, but it's actually pretty crazy. You see, in the 1930s, there was a man named Cleo McVickers who was a soap manufacturer. He invented the gooey substance in order to be a wallpaper cleaner. It worked well as a wall paper cleaner for 20 years or so until McVickers's son, Joseph, had the idea to take the wallpaper cleaner and use it as clay for preschoolers. Since it was gooey and doughy to the touch, he named it Play-Doh, and the rest is history. We've all grown up playing with the different colors of Play-Doh, of course being careful not to mix the colors.

Play-Doh's purpose changed over time. That's what we have to do as well. God will adjust your burdens and your calling as you begin to lean into them. Sure, he'll always use the gifts and abilities you have, but as your experiences change and as you learn and grow, you'll be tasked with a new calling and a new challenge. So, don't ever despise what may seem like interruptions in life. Oftentimes, the interruptions are indicators to the calling God is placing in front of you.

I'm convinced that our limited perspective is one of the greatest things holding us back from walking in our calling and being the switch in the world around us. We lose sight that all God wants from us is obedience in the now. So instead of being like Moses and Daniel and a host of other biblical heroes and walking in the now, we get caught up in what could happen in the future, what our plans are, and how much we want to accomplish. Whatever you're doing now, God wants to use it. Whatever you're going through, God is calling you through. Whatever the present presents, God is using it to do his work, right now. Wherever you've come from and wherever you're going, it's all a part of your calling.

So, work with all you have while God has you where you are. Believe in what he's called you to at your job, your school, and your life. Don't, however, limit your perspective so much that you lose sight that his plan for you is bigger and ever changing.

Don't get too comfortable, God has more work to do in and through you.

CHAPTER SEVEN
WALK IT OUT

Be strong and courageous. Do not be afraid or terrified because of them, for the LORD your God goes with you; he will never leave you nor forsake you." (Deut 31:6 NIV)

I'm a sports junkie. I love nearly all sports, but football and baseball are my absolute favorites. Give me an afternoon at home on a Saturday in October and I'm a happy camper. Give me a few MLB playoff games in October and I am a happy camper.

One of my favorite things about playing sports, and now watching sports as I've gotten older, is the back and forth. You know what I'm talking about. One team comes out in the first inning and hits two homers and many would just about call the game over even though it's the first inning. Baseball players and people who understand the game know that things can change on a dime. A few innings later, an error and some aggressive base running could lead to the other taking the lead. The bullpen of the now-leading team could then implode and switch the momentum right back. It's a back-and-forth, tug-of-war, kind of game.

All sports are full of ups and downs; that's why so many people love them. That's why professional sports are a multi–billion-dollar industry: people love the up and down, the give and take, the highs and lows. They love the thrill of a late-inning comeback or a Hail Mary touchdown pass. They love coming back after being down by what seemed like an insurmountable score.

Our callings and lives are much like that. As you and I begin to see God on the path he has for us and use our lives for more than just a 9-5 paycheck and weekend away from the office, we'll see ups and downs. When we begin to take our place in our lives with an attitude that we want to be used by God and we'll love others no matter what and we'll do things with more purpose, we'll experience a lot of highs and lows.

The Enemy of Calling

I spoke a few weeks ago with a friend who has struggled off and on with drug addiction since before he was an adult. His last fight with the addiction led him to the most extreme rehab facility he had ever been to. It was Christian based and extremely stringent. After graduating and getting out, my friend has lived an amazing, drug free life. He's recently begun to attend the church where I pastor and is even volunteering. During our conversation, he started talking about all of the things that had begun to happen to him during his three months out of rehab. As I listened to him talk about the ups and downs, I felt God wanted me to tell him that that's how his life is going to be. I told him that we have a real enemy who doesn't like when we begin to walk in new things and live in new ways. Ups and downs come because we have an adversary who reacts to our obedience.

My friend is not only overcoming his drug addiction, but he's also beginning to walk in his calling. He's beginning to talk more about his faith and live it out in front of his family and friends. That's when the enemy comes. He comes, not when you're living in the middle of mundane, but when you're on the cusp of a great calling.

The story of Nehemiah in Scripture is one that's often told in leadership circles and messages. In case you don't know the backstory, Nehemiah was the cupbearer for the king. He held a high position in the palace when he got word that the walls of his home nation of Jerusalem were in ruin. In those times, these walls represented so much to the people. It was a status symbol, a symbol of security and a practical protection for enemy armies. After hearing the news, Nehemiah talks to his king and gets permission to go back to Judah and help rebuild the walls. Nehemiah gathers a large team and they begin the work. The Bible says that, as the walls were about half up, some guys came who wanted to take them back down and take Nehemiah out.

That's an example of what often comes when we're being the switch. Here's Nehemiah leaving a place of status and security, stepping into his calling, and then the attack comes. As Christ followers being the switch, we are never promised an easy life or a life of pleasure. We are promised, however, significance, peace, and a life of purpose.

Seasons of Change

Every season of life brings new challenges, obstacles, victories, life, and pain. The more of life seasons I've gone through, the more I've come to appreciate each one. While no two seasons are the same, I've learned that just because it's not the same, that doesn't mean it's not as good. Seasons are just different.

Take, for instance, the actual seasons of the year. Each one transitions into the other. They each have good things about them and things that make us dread them. For the most part, if you asked people if they absolutely despised a season of the year, chances are they don't; they'd find the good and the bad in each.

Our callings are like that. Some seasons of our calling are fulfilling and full of victory. Other seasons are challenging and full of frustration and apparent failure. It's easy to live God's call when you're a pastor of a growing church and everything seems to be trending upward; it's another story when you work at a convenience store and you're trying to reach your coworkers and the store keeps getting robbed. Both are callings full of opportunity, but they each present unique opportunities and challenges.

But what do you do? What do you do when you're following God at your job, you're being the switch in your family, and you're working hard at getting that coworker to go to church with you, but it seems to be going nowhere? What do you do? God had some advice for Moses when Moses pushed back against what God had called him to do. Look at the exchange in Exodus 3:11–15.

> But Moses said to God, "Who am I that I should go to Pharaoh and bring the Israelites out of Egypt?" And God said, "I will be with you. And this will be the sign to you that it is I who have sent you: When you have brought the people out of Egypt, you will worship God on this mountain." Moses said to God, "Suppose I go to the Israelites and say to them, 'The God of your fathers has sent me to you,' and they ask me, 'What is his name?' Then what shall I tell them?" God said to Moses, "I am who I am. This is what you are to say to the Israelites: 'I am has sent me to you.'" God also said to Moses, "Say to the Israelites, 'The Lord, the God of your fathers—the God of Abraham, the God of Isaac and the God of Jacob—has sent me to you.

Did you catch the simplicity in God's response

to Moses's reaction? Basically, Moses is telling God that he can't do it, and God responds with a "Yeah, I know. That's why I'm doing it through you instead." Sometimes, just the power of knowing who's on our side can change everything about a situation. Just knowing your dad is at your side makes getting your first baseball hit a little easier. Knowing your Dad is beside you makes your haircut a little easier to deal with. Knowing your husband is by your side makes the pain of childbirth a little more bearable. Knowing your kids are by your side makes the divorce a little easier to swallow. A lot of our calling isn't about the perceived success or failure of that calling, but it's about who's with us as we're living it. God is with you. He's got you. Your job is obedience and surrender; His is presence and victory.

Have You Been There?

Each season of life, while both good and tough in certain ways, is made easier with someone by our side who's been through that season. When my wife and I were getting ready to have our first child, we talked to other parents. We didn't want to talk to a single guy in his 40s with no children (no offense), but we wanted to talk to a mom of three or four who's seen some stuff. We wanted advice from someone who's been there. When we bought our first home years ago, we wanted an experienced agent who would walk us through the process. As I counsel people, one of the greatest things I have to offer to them is my past experience with the same type of issues they are experiencing. That's why, in the struggles of living our calling on a daily basis, I believe David offers us so much when it comes to the ups and downs. He experienced them all. He had been there and done that. He experienced about every season of life we can imagine.

Throughout the remainder of this chapter, we'll talk a lot about the man who would eventually become King David, but we can't start there. His story of calling and being the switch starts long before he was king. Let's take a look at some of the lessons his life can teach us as we move forward with our life and our calling.

Being Forgotten Doesn't Make You a Failure

We've all been there, right? Maybe that's why you picked this book up. Maybe you feel like you've been forgotten and left out of doing anything significant in the kingdom of God. Maybe you've been forgotten by the people you thought would love you most. Maybe you've been feeling a call on your life, but you've been passed over for the opportunity to live out that calling.

David experienced being forgotten. David was a shepherd boy in the house of a father named Jesse. Jesse had eight sons, and one of them was deemed by God to be the second king of Israel, God's chosen nation. One day Samuel, the man to anoint the king, asked Jesse to line his boys up so they could discover the next king. After going through each brother who stood in front of him, Samuel asked Jesse if he had anymore. To that, Jesse responded, "There is still the youngest . . . he is tending the sheep" (1 Sam 16:11 NIV). He forgot David! Can you believe that? The calling that would eventually overwhelm David's life and transform a world was overlooked by his own father.

You are not a failure even if you've been passed

over. You are not a failure even if you feel like you're trying to be the switch but someone else keeps getting the platform. You are not a failure if you're trying to wait tables with excellence but someone else keeps getting the hours. You are not a failure. In fact, God has a history of using "forgotten" people. He can use you. He will use you. When we feel forgotten, we have to do what David did: act in humility and diligence. What do you do when you're getting looked over? You keep going. You keep trying. You keep being excellent.

Don't Let Success Lead to Your Failure

David continued to walk in humility even after his anointing that day from Samuel. In front of his other brothers, his dad Jesse, and Samuel, David was anointed king. Now, if you don't know the story, you probably think that David went right to the throne and started barking out orders. That's not what happened. Instead, David went back to the field. His job as shepherd wasn't over yet because the throne of Israel wasn't vacant yet. How difficult is that? To know where you're going and know you're called to it but it being unreachable?

Many would've quit right there and refused to go back to the stinky sheep after feeling the anointing of the oil. David didn't. He went back to the pasture and awaited his palace. Many of us have the same opportunity when we walk in our calling. The success we experience in being the switch and shedding light on Jesus will lead some to elevate us, but it will lead some of us to elevate ourselves. Don't let the success God gives you lead to the failure of your future. Keep being faithful in the call and context you find yourself now in until God opens new doors.

Don't Let the Page Dictate the Story

If you've been in Sunday school at all or maybe a Vacation Bible School, you know that David eventually would be called out from the field to the battlefield to check on his brothers. As he was checking on them, he heard the giant taunting his people and decided to do something about it. Before David steps up with his sling and stone, he asks a question: "Who is this uncircumcised Philistine that he should defy the armies of the living God?" (1 Sam 17:26 NIV). In other words, what's up with this? Why are you guys letting him intimidate you? Are you forgetting who your God is?

David didn't let what was in front of him determine where God would use him. We all need to remember this. Whoever you are in your calling or life, however you feel like you've failed or succeeded, where you are isn't all there is. There will be other days; there will be new opportunities; there will be times where you'll feel more useful. Don't let what people are saying to you and saying about you determine how much God will use you. There is more than you see. There is more for you to do than what appears obvious now.

In this scene David is saying, "Why are you letting the giant appear bigger than your God?" Why do we let what's around us appear bigger than the One that's within us? If he's called you to there, he'll get you through there.

Don't Despise What God Designed

Let's move the story of David and Goliath along a little. At this point David has talked Saul (the current king) into letting him fight Goliath. Basically, Saul gets to a point and kind of throws his hands up and says, "Go for it!" However, before David steps up to Goliath, Saul puts his own armor on David. Now, let's pause right there, because isn't that what many of us do with our calling? We see what someone else does and we want to look just like it. We see the way someone else parents and we try to parent our kids the same way. We see someone else start a Bible study in their home and we think our call should look the same way. We're really good at taking someone else's armor and stepping up to what we think we should do. Take note of this and highlight it: You were made to walk out your calling as you, not them. Don't despise it. Are you a single mom? Don't despise it. Are you bigger, smaller, taller, or shorter than them? Don't hate it; utilize it. Are you rich, poor, talkative, quiet, outgoing, introverted? Be you. God's designed you and your calling for you. Don't despise it.

If we skip the story ahead a little more, we see David taking this armor off, giving it back to Saul, telling him he can't fight in his stuff or do what he did. That takes guts! To give the king back his armor and pick up your sling and stone is harder than you'd ever imagine. Sometimes, though, denying other's expectations and stepping into your calling is the most important step.

Next, comes the biggest moment in David's life: "Then he took his staff in his hand, chose five smooth stones from the stream, put them in the pouch of his shepherd's bag and, with his sling in his hand, approached the Philistine" (1 Sam 17:40). Why did David choose stones, a shepherd's bag, and a sling? Because that's what shepherds do! That's what they know and are given. That's their sweet spot.

You have a sweet spot too. Understanding it, leaning into it, and developing it is one of the biggest things you can do to begin to be the switch. The way you're wired, your past, your frustrations, your victories, they all come to this point in your life. It's so you can walk in the calling of God. You're anointed and purposed on purpose by your loving Creator.

Don't Waste Your Time Chasing the Wrong Things

When we think about the animal kingdom, we don't usually think of a field mouse as having a leg up on a lion. At first glance, especially considering appearance, most of us would take a look at the field mouse and think it would never have a leg up on a lion. The truth is, it does. That's because lions know better than to chase field mice everywhere. In fact, as it turns out, hunting down and eating a field mouse would burn more calories than the mouse would provide it. If lions spent their entire time chasing and killing field mice, they'd starve to death. They would much rather chase, kill, and enjoy the calories of the antelope.

When it comes to your calling and the ups and downs, remember not to chase the field mice; instead, focus on the antelope. In other words, don't let the lows take you out as you try to compensate for a mistake or cover up something you think makes you less of a person or minister of the gospel. Don't chase the mice. Don't let the lies and the doubts take you away from your calling.

In the New Testament Too

Beyond just seeing David's call come to completion when he took the throne some fifteen years later, we see an example of overcoming the struggles in the New Testament too. Take a look at Paul. Paul was a man shipwrecked, snake bitten, and shaken for his faith but overwhelmingly effective in his call. Or what about Stephen? He was stoned to death but died a martyr's death because he was convinced of his call. He refused to live his life for just the here and now; he decided to be the switch in his day.

What about you? How will you respond when it doesn't go your way? Will you continue to seek God? Will you keep your face toward him, your ears in tune to him, and your calling pointed toward him? Don't chase mice; chase the antelope; chase God and the call He has for you.

CHAPTER EIGHT
BUT WHAT NOW?

Not that I have already obtained all this,
or have already arrived at my goal, but
I press on to take hold of that for which
Christ Jesus took hold of me. (Phil 3:12 NIV)

I've learned the value of slow progress while being a dad. When my little man was born, we didn't set him aside, pull up a chair, and begin to potty train him, teach him to ride a bike, buy him a car, and ask him to fill out college applications. That'd be crazy. Neither did we expect him to eat solid food the day he came out of the hospital or run to his room when he was in trouble.

No.

All of these lessons and milestones come little by little. He drank milk, and then slowly ate baby food, and then a little solid food, and now the boy can throw down some Taco Bell (I have no idea why we like Taco Bell so much). How did he get to eating tacos and quesadillas? He started small and made progress.

Start Somewhere

That's what it takes to be the switch as well. You aren't going to be perfect overnight. You probably aren't going to immediately see your life make complete sense and see revival in your neighborhood, though God can do that. You probably aren't going to see your entire office come to church the first time you invite them or see the other baristas you work with come to the Bible study the first time you have it. Don't get discouraged. Start little and dream big. Progress is better than paralysis. Start somewhere and keep going.

Just Imagine

Just imagine for a few moments...

You adopt this "be the switch" mindset now. You begin going to your job or to school with a different motive. You begin to be a person of integrity who lives out your faith. You find a deeper meaning in the things you do each and every day. You start to walk in the calling God intended for you. As you walk, you seek God and he begins to shape your life, not based off of where you want to end up but based on where he wants you now. You do that for the next ten years. Can you imagine what your life will look like? Can you imagine the attitude and zeal you approach those days with now that you have ten years of being the switch under your belt?

Moses wouldn't just go to Pharaoh and demand that his people get freed; he would lead the entire nation to the Jordan River and toward the Promised Land. Along the way the people would groan and moan and complain and sin. Moses would continue to lead them. At times he was their prophet and gave them the commandments to live by. He embraced the calling. At times he was their provider by giving them water from a rock. He embraced the calling. At times he was their warrior by raising his staff and letting God part the waters so that the Egyptian army would be defeated. He embraced the calling. Moses walked as the switch for much of his life. It never looked the same for very long. He was never in the same place for very long and, frankly, never experienced prolonged success. He'd go from a boy in a basket to a leader in limbo. He'd go from a guy with a speech problem to the spokesperson of the nation. God blessed him as he walked.

Every Body, One Body

One of the most beautiful things about the body of Christ is how we work together. That's why we need you being the switch where you live. You see, many people are attempting to save the world without helping to save their neighborhood. In 1 Corinthians 12 Paul talks about this concept in his famous illustration of the church as the Body of Christ.

> Just as a body, though one, has many parts, but all its many parts form one body, so it is with Christ. For we were all baptized by one Spirit so as to form one body—whether Jews or Gentiles, slave or free —and we were all given the one Spirit to drink. Even so the body is not made up of one part but of many.

What a beautiful passage of Scripture! It's the point of the church. The point is that we represent

Christ and serve the world. Whatever that looks like for you or me, it's up to us and God, but we work together. Imagine a world filled with believers in Jesus who are willing to put aside theological differences and work together as the body of Christ. You see, when I'm lifting weights with my arm (yeah, I actually do lift weights on occasion), my legs don't get mad because they aren't getting their turn. No; instead, I work out my entire body little by little so the entire thing can be in the best shape it possibly can. That's the body of Christ: stronger together and when everything is working. You be you, let them be them. We'll change the world.

Caution!

My caution for you as you begin to walk in your calling? Don't get numb to how God is using you. Don't lose sight of how God is using you, and treat every moment as an opportunity. I think it's easy, though, to get used to what God is doing in and through us. It's kind of like putting something in the slow cooker, sitting in the house all day, and never noticing the smell. In contrast, if someone else wasn't home when you put your dinner in the slow cooker and walked in after a few hours of it cooking, they'd notice the smell as soon as they walked in. When we're seeing something happen, the tendency is to get used to it and take it for granted. Don't take the fact that God is using your for granted. Don't go numb to what he's doing in and around you. I tell churches this all the time. Churches that are experiencing growth and new people meeting Jesus often forget how blessed they are. They are witnessing God moving week after week and fail to let it be new and exciting each time.

I often think about this idea of getting used to something when I travel. One of the worst parts without a doubt of flying is going through security and dealing with TSA (sorry if you're an agent, but we all think it). Now, I know they have a tough job. No one wants to deal with thousands of people a day who are often in a hurry and don't want to strip their shoes and belts in order to get to the real part of the airport. It's a tough job, but it's also a repetitive one. Day after day, hour after hour, they screen people as they show their boarding passes, pass through a check point, and grab their bags. It's a repetitive job and one they get used to, but it's not one that I want them to get tired of and overlook.

I want the TSA agent at the airport to be on their game every day, no matter how many days in a row they've worked or how many people they have patted down that day (yeah, that's always me for some reason). I want them to keep fresh and on task because my safety depends on it. They have important work to do.

Don't get used to the call you have. You have important work to do. Don't get used to all that God is doing and let it lead to your not appreciating what God is doing. Maintain your passion and refresh your spiritual life often. Continue to seek the face of God, even when things seem to be clicking, even when success seems to come often.

Make Time for What's Worth Your Time

How do you continue being the switch for years to come? It starts with setting your priorities. I've noticed something over my relatively short life: I make time for what I feel is worth my time. Make time to spend time with God. It could be in the morning, it may be on your lunch break, it may even be before you go to bed, but do something to let God work in you. Something happens when we get alone with God. We begin to see things as he sees them and we continue to walk in our calling, no matter how tough it gets.

Make time to spend time with God, but also make time to intentionally serve him by serving others. When we make the time rather than just letting it all happen in the moment, we make it a priority to have our fire stoked more often. When we're committed to serving a charity, our church, or a non-profit, we're prioritizing our calling and reminding ourselves how much it matters. Oftentimes when we prioritize and are intentional about a particular thing happening, the bigger moments happen easier too. Suddenly, it's easier for us to recognize God opportunities in our lives.

Let's Do It!

What's left? Just for us to allow ourselves to be flipped and start shinning for Jesus. Just for us to make some small adjustments and mindset changes in order to be the best we can be for God and against the kingdom of darkness.

Initiate the change.

Live your calling.

Too much depends on it.

Be the switch.

CONCLUSION

SEARCHING FOR THE SWITCH

When I set out to write this book, my hope wasn't that it'd be another book you half read, gain a few insights, put on a shelf, and never pick back up. In fact, I don't want that at all. I want this book to be transformative for you. I want it to be something you bookmark on your e-reader and highlight in the pages as you read in your bed. I want it to be a resource for you to refer to when you feel purposeless and passionless. I want it to be something you go back to when the work seems endless and mundane, when you feel trapped by life, when parenting feels more like refereeing, and when your career feels most like a job.

With that in mind, this may be your favorite chapter of this book. I've added some ideas to help you and I start being the switch in our lives. The following questions and declarations will help you set your focus as you live your calling and live your life.

Questions

To help make things a little more practical, I think we can always ask questions. Questions that will help us take a deeper look and reevaluate our lives. Questions, especially those we ask of ourselves, have the power to help us think through things, pray more specific prayers, and bring passion back to our lives.

Below is a list of questions to ask yourself when you need to. Feel free to take a photo, copy and paste, or highlight so you can refer back often. This may even become a part of your time with God for several weeks as you try to recover passion and be the switch to your family, friends, colleagues, peers, and circle.

Where is the opportunity in what I currently see as an obstacle?

Who's one person God has put in my life that I can encourage?

What could be God's purpose in having me "on the far side?"

Do I shine light on the world more by how I walk or with how I talk?

What lies are Satan whispering to me about my purpose that I need to call out and replace with truth?

Am I more focused on seeking God or manipulating him into fixing my life?

If I'm the only Jesus follower the people around me meet, are they likely to want to know Jesus?

Do I have margin in my life for divine interruptions and opportunities to serve others? How can I get it?

Do I see my children as a gift to steward? Am I being intentional with them lately?

Is my spouse a priority?

How have I seen God bless as I've been more focused on being the switch where I live? How is he honoring me as I honor Him?

Do I regularly recognize the action of God in my life?

Am I part of a local church body? Why or why not?

Is God birthing a calling in what I consider a nuisance?

What new things are exciting me? Is this pointing toward a new calling?

What new gifts does God seem to be instilling in me for his purposes?

Who can I text that may need encouragement?

How am I helping serve the body at my local church? What areas could they use help that may help me be a switch as well?

Who can I invite to my church?

Have I been a person of excellence lately? Am I shining the love of Jesus by the way I work?

How's my integrity level lately?

Am I being the switch?

Declarations

One of the practices I began about five years ago is speaking certain declarations out loud regularly over my life. It may seem odd, but somehow, speaking them out loud and hearing them makes me more convinced of them. I also think there's something powerful about the words of a Christ follower. There's something about speaking truth out loud that I believe sets the record straight with our enemy and sets the records straight in our minds.

These are truths that you probably know, but sometimes need to be reminded of. They aren't ground breaking and probably won't blow your mind by their deep theological truth, but they are true and, I think, they'll help you stay focused on truth, Christ, and your calling.

I am created in the image of my Creator.

I have a purpose in being where I am.

My past does not define me.

I love people and believe the best about others.

I remain positive, no matter how negativity presents itself.

I am anointed and empowered by the living God to do what he's called me to do.

My calling is for me but isn't about me. I'll walk in selflessness and service.

The supremacy of Christ is so much greater than the severity of my problems.

God is always making things better and better in my life.

I do not just live life as it comes; I come at life with purpose and passion.

I am the switch and I will help change the world with Jesus's power at work in me.

36312491R00081

Made in the USA
Columbia, SC
24 November 2018